On North Eastern Lines

Derek Huntriss

First published 1998

ISBN 0 7110 2543 6

Published by Ian Allan Publishing

An imprint of Ian Allan Ltd, Terminal House, Station Approach,
Shepperton, Surrey TW17 8AS; and printed by Ian Allan Printing Ltd.,
Coombelands House, Coombelands Lane, Addlestone, Weybridge,
Surrey KT15 1HY.

Code: 9801/B3

Front Cover: Class A8 4-6-2T No 69861 climbs the
1 in 49 from Grosmont to Goathland near Beckhole with
a Whitby to Malton local in April 1954. The consist
includes a former North Eastern Railway brake
composite.   *J. M. Jarvis*

Rear Cover: NCB Philadelphia's 'Lambton Tank'
0-6-2T No 42 heads a loaded coal train for Sunderland
through the station at Pallion on 20 September 1961.
Passenger services from Pallion were withdrawn on
4 May 1964.   *G. M. Staddon*

This Page: On the last day of BR steam operations in
the northeast, 9 September 1967, Class Q6 0-8-0
No 63395 passes Ryhope with empties from Sunderland.
Paul Riley

Introduction

Not forgetting the pioneering achievements of Richard Trevithick with his early locomotives, it could be said that the cradle of the railways was the northeast of England. Early waggonways in the region can be traced back to c.1605, the northeast adopting the true railway system of flanged wheel and edge rail in preference to the plateway design.

The North Eastern Railway, like most large railways, was formed from an amalgamation of smaller companies and naturally it was started with a hotch-potch of locomotives. Eventually the company was to own some 2,000 engines and was next in size to the LNWR, Midland and GWR and had the monopoly of the northeast with its important mineral and industrial traffic. Having said that the NER's passenger traffic cannot be overlooked. This was also of considerable importance because, in addition to the through traffic on the East Coast route, there were numerous secondary routes and branch lines which, by contemporary standards, gave excellent service. The proud boast of the NER in the first decade of the present century was that it had 'The Fastest Train in the British Empire', the ideal course from York to Darlington being perfectly aligned in favour of the locomotive. So successful were the NER's locomotive designs that Wilson Wordsell's 1906 designed Class P3 0-6-0 (LNER Class J27) together with Raven's Class T2 0-8-0s (LNER Class Q6) were still in operation when BR steam operations in the northeast ceased in September 1967. In fact these two classes were the last examples of pre-Grouping steam locomotives to operate anywhere on BR.

Today the changes and cutbacks in the northeast's industry and railways have had the knock on effect of rising unemployment which rivals the depression of the 1930s.

Here, this title takes the reader back to the halcyon days of the 1950s and 1960s when the dedicated photographers, whose work makes up this title, were able to witness the dying rays of the industrial sunset over some of the northeast's scenes of rough beauty. The title takes the reader on a brief journey down the East Coast route from York to Berwick and, in a general southerly direction, sets out to examine some of the secondary, branch and mineral routes whose intricate tapestry was interwoven throughout the region. To add meaning to the title, pictures of industrial workings have been included as well as the Rothbury branch of the former North British Railway over whose metals a number of former NER locomotives worked.

Bibliography

W. Philip Conolly: *British Railways Pre-Grouping Atlas & Gazetteer;* Ian Allan

Peter Cookson & John E. Farline: *LNER Lines in the Yorkshire Ridings;* Challenger Publications

P.B. Hands: *Whatever Happened to Steam Vols. 1 -30;* P. B. Hands

Chris Hawkins, John Hooper & George Reeve: *British Railways Engine Sheds - an LNER inheritance;* Irwell Press

K.Hoole: *A Regional History of the Railways of Great Britain — Vol 4 The North East;* David & Charles

Keith R. Pirt: *Real Steam in Colour Vol. 1 York;* Norseman Publications

Peter J. Robinson & Ken Groundwater: *British Railways Past & Present No 4 The North East;* Silver Link Publishing

Alan R. Thompson & Ken Groundwater: *British Railways Past & Present No 11 North Yorkshire (Part 1) York & Selby, the Dales, & Skipton to Garsdale;* Silver Link Publishing

Nigel Trevena: *Steam For Scrap Vols 1 & 2;* Atlantic Transport Publishers

Ian L. Wright: *Branch Line Byways Vol 4 London & North Eastern;* Atlantic Transport Publishers

W. Yeadon: *Yeadon's Register of LNER Locomotives Vols 1 - 10;* Challenger Publications

Magazines: *Backtrack; Modern Railways; Railway Bylines; Railway Magazine; Railway World; Steam World; The World of Trains; Trains Illustrated.*

Acknowledgements

The author offers his sincere thanks to the many dedicated photographers whose work appears in these pages.

In addition to these photographers, I must also offer my thanks to fellow authors Alan Thompson and Ken Groundwater for sharing their in-depth knowledge of the subject in addition to allowing me access to photographs in the J. W. Armstrong Trust Collection. Sincere thanks are also given to Brian Stevens for his efforts in fine tuning my scribbling, of this and eight previous titles.

Derek Huntriss

Camborne, Cornwall
November 1997

The North Eastern Railway coat of arms as applied to apple-green liveried Class J72 0-6-0 No 68736, seen at York station on 7 September 1960. The last two survivors of this class, Nos 69005 and 69023 had been withdrawn in October 1965, but had avoided the journey to the scrapyard by being transferred into departmental service. No 69023 finally being saved by Mr Roland Ainsworth of Leeds.

Trevor B. Owen

Left: Hull Dairycoates (53A) MPD's WD 2-8-0 No 90378 accelerates a heavy southbound freight past Dringhouses Yard at York in October 1959. Situated south of York, Dringhouses Yard had been ripe for modernisation at the end of the 1950s when authorisation for semi-automatic hump shunting of block sections was given, the remodelled yard opening in 1961. However, the dramatic turnaround of rail freight from common user to block load only traffic in the 1980s sounded its death knell. The yard remained operational until April 1987 when the Rowntree-Mackintosh operation switched from rail traffic to juggernauts. Today the hump yard is levelled although it has seen use by the Civil Engineer's Department to stockpile up to 3,000 tons of spoilt ballast after the 1989 remodelling. *D. Penney*

Above: Summer Saturdays in the 1950s could be relied upon to produce a steady stream of excursion traffic to Scarborough and the Yorkshire coast resorts, from the West Riding of Yorkshire, Lancashire and the North Midlands, much of it being handled by unrebuilt 'B16' 4-6-0s. Here 'B16' No 61452 waits for its next duty at York station in 1959. *D. Penney*

5

Above: York station pilot, Class J72 0-6-0T No 68677 is seen at the south end of the station in October 1959. Allocated to York MPD when new in December 1898 as NER No 1746, it was initially employed on freight shunting duties. Upon Nationalisation in 1948 it was given the number 68677 and was fitted with vacuum brakes enabling it to work passenger stock. *D. Penney*

Right: By October 1964 York (50A) MPD had an allocation of no fewer than 14 Class A1 Pacifics, many of them with little or no work. Here, No 60124 *Kenilworth* is seen at York and is still immaculate five months after receiving a General Repair at Darlington. One of the first batch built at Doncaster, No 60124 was fitted with a Flaman speed recorder driven from the

right hand coupling pin. This device was removed during 1950-51 although she kept the supporting bracket for nearly 10 years. After several accidents involving this batch of locos in the 1950s inspectors concluded that the drivers had misjudged their speed and by May 1963 all 'A1' Pacifics were fitted with Smith-Stone speed indicators. *D. Penney*

This charming picture taken at Alne on 2 June 1957 depicts members of the Branch Line Society taking a last look at Class J71 No 68726 operating the branch service to Easingwold, their tour having arrived at Alne behind Class D20 No 62387. This 2½-mile long branch was opened on 27 July 1891 and cost £17,000 to construct. When the railway purchased a second engine in 1903 the first was sold and when the locomotive was under repair a second engine had to be hired from the NER or LNER. Eventually ex-NER locomotives of Classes J71 or J72 completely took over the working although engines of both of these classes could not be accommodated in the tiny engine shed at Easingwold. Having operated with a light railway licence since 1928 the branch remained privately owned beyond Nationalisation. The last train, conveying freight and parcels, ran on 27 December 1957.

E. E. Smith / J. W. Armstrong Trust Collection

Class D20 4-4-0 No 62360 is seen at Northallerton with the SLS/MLS 'Northern Dales' railtour on 4 September 1955. The train had been brought from Darlington via Eaglescliffe by Class A8 4-6-2T No 69855 which then piloted No 62360 through Wensleydale to Hawes. During the summer of 1954 Gateshead (52A) MPD's 'D20' 4-4-0s had been regularly used on Newcastle to Middlesbrough expresses, much to the displeasure of the engine crews who considered them to be 'worn out'. No 62360 was the most consistent performer.

K. H. Cockerill/J. W. Armstrong Trust Collection

Left: Class A3 Pacific No 60075 *St. Frusquin* waits by the turntable at Darlington (51A) MPD in September 1963 as Class K1 No 62004 is being turned. In May 1948, when BR were in the experimental stage of choosing a standard livery, No 60075 was chosen to be painted in a purple/blue colour and was unusual in having the red and cream lining also applied to the casing of the outside cylinders and valves.   *G. Rixon*

Above: Ivatt Class 4 No 43129 heads the RCTS/SLS 'North Eastern' railtour across the East Coast main line at S&D Crossing on 30 September 1963. When the Newcastle & Darlington Junction Railway was completed on 18 June 1844 the famous level crossing north of Parkgate Junction was brought into use. This crossing has now been removed but in the beginning the first NER rule book gave strict instructions that 'the

coal and mineral trains are invariably to give way to the passing of passenger trains'. Every driver had to 'sound his whistle' at least ½-mile before reaching the crossing, and continue to do so until he had got the attention of the signalman. Drivers who chose to disregard these rules had to be reported and 'signalman to be liable to a fine of Five Shillings in every case in which he shall omit to report any driver'.   *R. Hobbs*

Above: Stanier 2-8-0 No 48712 is seen in the Darlington North Road Works yard after repair on 27 March 1965. Following the restriction of Derby and Doncaster Works to diesel traction in 1963, Darlington took over the responsibility of steam locomotive repair on a large scale. Of those to come under the care of Darlington were 172 WD 2-8-0s formerly maintained at Crewe and 739 locomotives maintained at Doncaster, including all types of LNER Pacific, 'B1s', 'K1s', 'O1s', 'O4s', 'V2s' and WD 2-8-0s. In addition to these there were 828 locomotives once maintained at Derby, this total including BR 4-6-0s of Classes 4 and 5 , LMS 2-6-4Ts, Class 8F 2-8-0s, Classes 2F, 3F and 4F 0-6-0s, Class 0F 0-6-0Ts and 0-4-0STs. *G.M. Staddon*

Right: Waiting for the cutter's torch in Darlington scrap line on 13 May 1962 are three former NER Class J72 0-6-0s including Nos 68729 and 68688. The onslaught of dieselisation had brought many former LNER types to the yard: Class D49 4-4-0s, V1 and V3 2-6-2Ts, J39 0-6-0s, etc., not to mention the long-lived NER 'J27' 0-6-0s, 'Q6' 0-8-0s and 'B16' 4-6-0s. *K. Fairey*

Darlington (51A) MPD's Class K1 2-6-0 No 62004 heads a down freight at Aycliffe on 5 May 1962. No 62004 was one of 70 Class K1 mixed traffic 2-6-0s, designed by A.H. Peppercorn as a development of Class K1/1, built by the North British Locomotive Co Ltd, Glasgow, in 1949 and 1950. This class saw wide ranging service in the Scottish, Eastern and North Eastern Regions of British Railways from Mallaig in the north to March in the south. Happily sister locomotive No 62005 was preserved by the North Eastern Locomotive Preservation Group. She was the natural choice for preservation having received a general overhaul at Darlington Works in January 1965, running some 74,000 miles after its previous out-shopping from Doncaster in February 1961. As for No 62004, she was reallocated to West Hartlepool (51C) MPD in December 1964 where she survived until withdrawn in December 1966.   *G.M. Staddon*

14

Air-pump fitted BR Standard Class 9F 2-10-0
No 92061 approaches Tyne Yard with an up tank
train on 16 September 1963. The practice of using
Tyne Dock (52H) MPD's Class 9Fs for other duties
was not uncommon when they were waiting for the
arrival of an ore shipment. When Heaton (52B) MPD
was pushed for motive power the 2-10-0s would be
used on freights to Tweedmouth and Edinburgh.
No 92098 was seen on a southbound fitted freight at
Harrogate which was usually a Gateshead Class V2 or
Pacific duty.

In the background of the picture is the
Ravensworth Shop Pit located adjacent to the yard
exit, and closed in 1962.

The Tyne Dock-Consett ore trains were tailor-
made for the BR Class 9F 2-10-0s, seven such locomotives, Nos 92060-6, being fitted with
Westinghouse pumps and allocated new to Tyne
Dock shed in 1955. These were supplemented in 1956
by Nos 92097-9. The use of these engines allowed an
extra wagon in the train loadings and made life much
easier for the crews; particularly appreciated was the
more comfortable cab, affording much better protec-
tion from the elements, particularly in winter.

G.M. Staddon

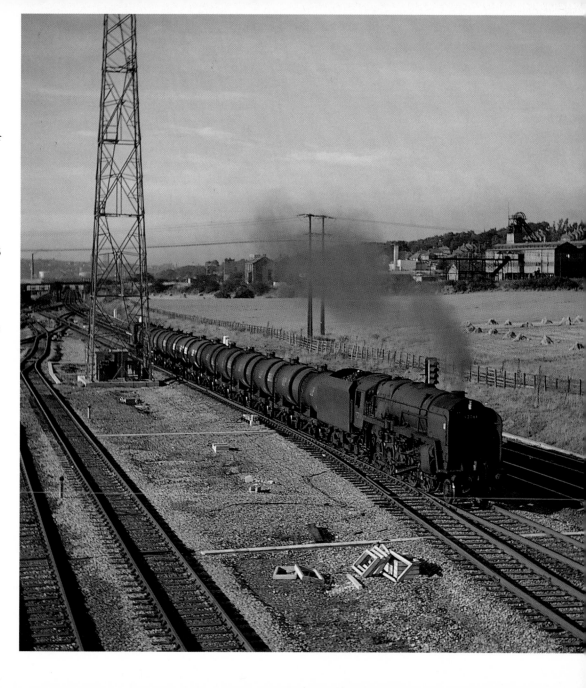

Left: This view of the King Edward VII Bridge taken in the mid-1950s shows an unidentified Class Q6 0-8-0 crossing on to the Durham side with a short freight bound for Low Fell mineral exchange sidings. The red brick building in the foreground is the site of the first Tyneside terminus of the Newcastle & Carlisle Railway company, the first trans-Pennine route to be opened. On this unlikely site was Redheugh station, the point from which travellers would wait for the ferry to complete their journey to Newcastle. The shipbreaking yard adjacent to Redheugh jetty was that belonging to Messrs King & Co, their rail-mounted cranes utilised some original N&C metals. King's broke up everything from World War I submarines, steam paddle tugs to WW2 escort destroyers and as in this view, small Dutch coasters. *E. E. Smith/K. Groundwater Collection*

Above: Another mid-1950s view taken from the east end of Newcastle Central station depicting an unidentified Class J72 0-6-0T going about its duties as station pilot. A 1960 scheme returned two members of the class to the old NER livery, the engines concerned being Gateshead (52A) MPD's No 68723 and York (50A) MPD's No 68736.

K. H. Cockerill/J. W. Armstrong Trust Collection

17

Above: This wintry view, taken c1957, depicts an unidentified Class A1 Pacific as it leaves the east end of Newcastle Central station for Heaton (52B) MPD. To the right, a Class B1 4-6-0 approaches with a heavy freight. To the left are the bay platforms for destinations to both Northumberland and Durham coastal resorts and ahead is the old Castle Keep beyond the diamond crossing. Perched high above the junction points is the No 1 signalbox; this was removed in the wake of the 1959 resignalling scheme that was to see the removal of the large gantries spectacularly bristling with semaphore signals. The new power box, opened in April 1959, took over the work of four older-type signalboxes and, after an extension in 1964, the work of seven more mechanical lever-type boxes at Manors North, Jesmond, West Jesmond, Argyle Street, Ouseburn, Riverside and Heaton Station. The famous diamond crossing went through many slimming sessions between 1959 and today as the bay feeders were given reduced access to the High Level Bridge and it finally became a simple junction in 1990 following the introduction of IECC solid state interlocking throughout the Newcastle area. The platform on which the photographer was standing has also undergone radical alterations as it was heightened, lengthened and re-profiled ready for the introduction of the main line electric services which began in 1992.

E. E. Smith/K. Groundwater Collection

Right: A once common sight in the mid-1950s as Haymarket (64A) MPD's Class A2 Pacific No 60509 *Waverley* has arrived at the west end of Newcastle Central with the up 'Heart of Midlothian' and stands in platform 8. Waiting in platform 11 is an unidentified Class A3 Pacific together with an additional coach. The Grantham-based loco is waiting to take the train forward. The up train was allowed a maximum of no more than 400 tons for two reasons. Many speed restrictions existed on the main line after World War 2 and Class A2 motive power could not always be guaranteed. Thus, south of Newcastle, the permissible load rose to 450 tons, hence the additional coach.

E. E. Smith/K. Groundwater Collection

Left: This superb view taken on 29 September 1963 depicts Ivatt Class 4 2-6-0 No 43057 crossing Ouseburn viaduct, north of Newcastle, with the RCTS 'North Eastern Railtour' as it makes for the Riverside line to Percy Main. Here the train was assisted by sister loco No 43129 for the journey over the Tyne Improvements Commission's line to Tyne Commission Quay. *Roy Hobbs*

Above: Heaton (52B) MPD's Class A1 Pacific No 60129 *Guy Mannering* gets under way after leaving Beal with the 2.25pm Edinburgh (Waverley) to Newcastle stopping train on 31 May 1962. The opening of a new power signalbox at Belford in 1962 completed a continuous section of colour-light signalling between Alnmouth and Burnmouth. The new box took over the work of a gantry-type signal box at Belford, which had

51 levers and a gate wheel, and a cabin at Crag Mill which had 25 levers and a gate wheel. Earlier that year the North Eastern Region had opened a new power box at Tweedmouth which had replaced four mechanical boxes at Marshall Meadows, Berwick, Tweedmouth North and Tweedmouth South. This box was situated at the junction of the East Coast main line and the branch to Coldstream. *M. Mensing*

21

BR Standard Class 2 2-6-0 No 78049 approaches Berwick over the Royal Border Bridge with the 4pm branch service from St Boswells on 25 May 1962. Whilst the actual border between England and Scotland was at a bleak point on the clifftop near Marshalls Meadow, the outstanding landmark at Berwick must rank as one of the best known and most elegant Victorian railway structures in the country. Carrying Anglo-Scottish traffic across the Tweed, its elevation provided panoramic views of the Northumberland coastline. Prior to construction of Stephenson's railway bridge, passengers bound for Newcastle left the train at Berwick station and were transported by coach for the remainder of the 60-mile journey. It is interesting to note that during planning for electrification of the route it was suggested that there should be a break in the catenary to prevent the harmful visual impact, trains having to coast across without power! *M. Mensing*

Tender-first Class K1 2-6-0 No 62021 departs from Alnwick with the branch train for Alnmouth in June 1966. Steam working on the three-mile branch was discontinued from June 18 1963, the K1 Class 2-6-0s being sent to Blyth to replace the ageing Class J27 0-6-0s. The following day services were taken over by two-car diesel-multiple units, these surviving until the branch closed on 29 January 1968. The terminus at Alnwick was opened in 1850 and rebuilt in 1887 when the North Eastern Railway completed the line to Coldstream.

Roy Hobbs

Below: Class J27 0-6-0 No 65891 shunts the yard at Scotsgap during its return from the Rothbury branch, prior to departure for Morpeth during the last week of operation in November 1963. The Wansbeck Valley line ran from Morpeth to Reedsmouth Junction where it met the Border Counties line from Riccarton Junction to Hexham. Both lines represented the southernmost operation of the former North British Railway.

Right: Another view of No 65891 earlier on the same day as it traverses the bleak moorland countryside on its return from Rothbury to Scotsgap Junction. A feature of operations on this line in the mid-1950s was British Railways' 'Garden Specials', circular tours from Newcastle Central which visited Hexham, Reedsmouth, Bellingham, Scotsgap, Rothbury and Morpeth by a series of reversing manoeuvres. The main purpose of these trips was to view the station gardens which were invariably well looked after despite the fact that some of the stations had closed to passenger traffic. Although being closed, some of these stations had won prizes in competitions organised by the railway. In addition to calling at the above named stations, stops were also made at Stocksfield, Riding Mill, Corbridge, Humshaugh and Wark.   *Both: Roy Hobbs*

Left: Class J27 0-6-0 No 65893 threads the spoil heaps as it crosses NCB metals with empties for the Ashington Colliery complex. The coal companies' internal railway, approximately 20 miles in length, was the largest system in Northumberland and operated a private passenger service to take miners to and from the pit-heads and back to the baths at the end of shifts.

Above: Here NCB 0-6-0T No 40 is seen with a miners' train at Ashington in March 1966. These trains, which comprised ancient stock hauled by an assortment of tank engine shunters, could often be seen bowling along with carriage doors swinging open. These trains were of two distinct types: 'Clean' for taking miners to the pit-heads at the start of shifts and 'Dirty' for end of

shift trips to the baths. The end of this fascinating private rail complex came in December 1986 when the ex-BR Class 14 diesel-hydraulic shunters were withdrawn, much to the regret of those who remember the mixed assortment of engines and GNR or NER coaches.

Both: Alan Jarvis

With miners' cottages visible from one end of the horizon to the other, Class J27 0-6-0 No 65842 heads a loaded coal train near Winning in March 1966. By 1886 the Ashington collieries had obtained an outlet to the east by building a line to connect with the former Blyth & Tyne Railway at a point where the Newbiggin branch turned away eastwards from the uncompleted Warkworth Extension. Additional coal staithes were opened at Blyth in 1888 and a second line connecting with the south end of the new staithes was opened from Newsham to Blyth. The next development in the port of Blyth came in 1893 when the Cambois branch of 1867 was widened and extended, a direct route for Ashington coals being provided with an additional curve at the junction with the Bedlington to Newbiggin line (Marchey's House junction to Winning junction). Opened on 13 July 1896 these extensions meant that coal from Ashington could reach Blyth without a single reversal being necessary. Work was started of further staiths before World War 1 but was suspended until 1926 and completed by April 1928.   *A. Jarvis*

With coal stacked high on its tender Class J27 0-6-0 No 65838 simmers outside South Blyth (52F) MPD on 20 September 1963. Over 6,000,000 tons of coal a year were shipped at Blyth in the 1930s, a total surpassed in 1961 when 6,889,317 tons were 'teemed' — an expression describing the unloading of coal into the holds of ships. The expansion at Blyth resulted in less traffic being moved from the Tyne, the longer journey adding to the cost of the coal. In fact, when Blyth was in full operation 90 per cent of the coal shipped through the port was mined from collieries within a six-mile radius. *Ken Fairey*

Left: This splendid view taken in 1954 catches the fireman of Tyne Improvement Commission's No 7 putting his feet up between duties. This 0-6-0, Works No 1704, built by Hunslet in 1937, had been operated by Sir Lindsay Parkinson, contractor, until 1949, and survived at TIC until February 1958 when it was scrapped. Albert Edward Dock is in the background.

Above: The crew of Tyne Improvement Commission's No 11 pose for the camera again in 1954. This venerable machine, delivered new to TIC as Robert Stephenson No. 3072 in 1901 is standing in the loco shed area of the dock. Like No 7, No 11 lasted until 1958, finally meeting the cutter's torch in April of that year. *Both: D. G. Charlton*

Above: This rare view, taken on 18 July 1945, was copied from a Dufaycolor original and depicts Black Hawthorn 0-6-0T No 888 *Burnhopeside* of 1887 at Craghead Colliery. This colliery was owned by Holmside and South Moor Collieries Ltd and became part of the National Coal Board's No 6 Area on 1 January 1947. The loco, rebuilt by Hawthorn Leslie in 1931, was scrapped in September 1959. *J. M. Jarvis*

Right: Also in the NCB's No 6 Area is Robert Stephenson 0-6-0 No 2847 of 1896 at Victoria Garesfield Colliery. Delivered new to Priestman Collieries Ltd as Victoria No 4 it became No 1 in the NCB's No 6 Area numbering system and survived until October 1962.

F. R. Bell/J.W. Armstrong Trust Collection

Left: Tender-first Class Q6 0-8-0 No 63431 heads a rake of coal empties through the station at Pelaw on 24 May 1967. At Pelaw, on the line from Middlesbrough to Newcastle, lines joined from the left and the right, the former being the connection from Washington, and the latter from South Shields.   *Ken Fairey*

Above: Former NER 0-6-2T, BR Class N10 No 69097 propels a single wagon up the incline at Lobley Hill on 8 September 1960. This regular Saturday turn against the general run of coal traffic was to deliver household coal to the pit village. Depending on the load, one or two Class N10s would propel one or two 21-ton hopper wagons, no use being made of the self-acting inclines. As there was a section of 1 in 11 on Baker's Bank, this would rank as the steepest adhesion worked bank in the country. Today a section of incline on the Bowes Railway from Blackham's Hill to Black Fell survives in preservation.   *Trevor B. Owen*

Below: An unidentified Class Q7 0-8-0 heads a north-bound freight over the Durham Junction Railway's Victoria Bridge between Penshaw and Washington. This structure, which survives today as a listed building, was designed by the eminent railway engineer, T. E. Harrison. It has four arches with an overall length of about 800ft, a height of about 135ft. Another structure on which he worked together with Robert Stephenson was the High Level Bridge spanning the Tyne between Newcastle and Gateshead.

Right: Class Q6 0-8-0 No 63459 marshals a train from Stella Gill sidings at South Pelaw Junction near Chester-le-Street on 18 September 1966. The train, once complete, left for its final destination at Consett.
Both: G.M. Staddon

Left: This view, taken in the mid-1950s, shows Andrew Barclay Works No 2078 of 1939 at work in the steel-works at Consett as Consett Iron Co 'B' No 12. Established in 1864, the Consett Iron Co originally drew its resources locally from Cleveland and latterly from Spain when local iron ore deposits became worked out. After the Stanhope & Tyne Railway failed in late 1840 alternative routes had to be opened to satisfy supply and demand. Coal was initially supplied locally from about six different collieries and the limestone, which was needed for flux, came from Stanhope. With massive transport costs, the works and its busy railway arteries closed finally in 1983, the railway playing a final sad role as the works was broken up — it was taken away by train to Sheffield to be smelted, the last load going 'down the bank' on 14 September 1983. *D. G. Charlton*

Above: Specially reinstated from withdrawn stock to work the RCTS 'North Eastern Railtour', Class Q7 0-8-0 No 63460 is seen at Consett on 28 September 1963. The train, headed by No 63460, had left Newcastle Central for Tyne Dock at 8.45am before tackling the route taken by the iron ore trains to Consett. Class K1 No 62027 worked to Waskerley then No 63460 took over to West Auckland. *R. Hobbs*

A 1954 view of operations on the Tyne Dock to Consett route as Class O1 No 63755 heads a loaded ore train through Beamish Woods with Beamish Colliery in the background. To work these trains, which were introduced in November 1953, 10 locomotives were fitted with Westinghouse pumps and air reservoirs.

These engines were of two classes, the rebuilt GC 2-8-0s of Class O1 (Nos 63712/55/60, 63856/74) and the three-cylinder NER Class Q7 0-8-0s (Nos 63460/3/5/9/73). The 'O1s' were employed as train engines, the 'Q7s' mainly as bankers. The 10 engines represented the minimum required to operate the

services which began with 10 trains a day but, which in June 1954, were expanded to 14 trains a day round the clock. Banking engines made three round trips from Pelaw South to South Medomsley before returning to Tyne Dock for coal, water and re-manning. Train engines returned after every trip. *D. G. Charlton*

When a Class O1 was not available for duties to Consett a Class Q7 0-8-0 was used as train engine, and another of the same class without pumps could be used as banker from Pelaw South. Here a Class Q7 is hard at work near Ox Hill in August 1956. In an eight hour-shift crews had to prepare their engines, make a round trip to Consett and dispose of their engines before signing off. The time allowed from Tyne Dock to Consett was 111min. *D. G. Charlton*

41

Above: Class 9F 2-10-0 No 92061, ably assisted by Class O1 No 63856, pounds up the grade west of Annfield Plain near Greencroft with an ore train for Consett on 8 September 1960. The 2-10-0s came new from Crewe Works to Consett, Nos 92060-6 in November/ December 1955 and Nos 92097-9 in June/ July 1956. However, after only a month or so, there was a severe motive power shortage on the Midland main line and seven were reallocated to Wellingborough, Westhouses and Toton, drifting back some four to six months later. Whilst availability of the '9Fs' was generally good,

there were periods of boiler problems and in April 1964 only two were available for traffic, York (50A) MPD relieving the crisis with the loan of No 92006 for banking duties. With the headlong rush into dieselisation, the Tyne Dock 2-10-0s had all departed by the end of 1966, nine to the scrapyard and one, No 92065, to Wakefield (56A) MPD where it enjoyed a brief final fling in the South Yorkshire coalfield with the odd trip into the Midlands.

Trevor B. Owen

Right: Class 9F No 92065 is seen on home territory passing Tyne Dock (52H) MPD in March 1966. Before the arrival of diesels for the Tyne Dock to Consett ore trains an experiment was begun in May 1962 with one of Saltley (21A) MPD's mechanical stoker-fitted 2-10-0s, No 92167. Specially prepared small coal had to be provided as larger lumps could not be handled by the stoker 'worm'. The combination of this small coal and heavy-handed firing due to inexperience produced some volcanic smoke effects.

Alan Jarvis

An unusual view, taken from the top of the storage bunkers at Tyne Dock, shows No 92098 pushing empties into the loading plant on 9 July 1960. The steel hoppers, each of which had two separate compartments, discharged by four side-opening doors to each wagon. Opening and closing the side doors was achieved by four compressed air engines, the doors of each compartment having two engines, one at either end. Each compressed air engine had two cylinders, one of 16in. diameter and one of 14in, the piston rods of each cylinder being connected by levers to the doors. When the doors were in the closed position they were kept that way by the action of the 14in cylinder which was maintained at a constant air pressure of 85psi. This pressure provided by two 10in. Westinghouse pumps on the locomotive was sustained through the train by the 'constant pressure' air pipe. There were also manually-operated safety locks which had to be released before the doors could be opened.

After these locks had been released the doors were opened by allowing air-pressure to enter the 16in diameter cylinders on the wagons.

Trevor B. Owen

The last survivor of ex-NER Class T1 4-8-0T, No 69921, a Wilson Worsdell design of 1909, is depicted outside Tyne Dock (52H) MPD on 7 September 1960. Having one of the least common wheel arrangements on the British locomotive scene, 15 engines of the type were built at Gateshead for the North Eastern Railway in 1909-10 were designated Class X in the NER's classification. They were designed to provide a powerful shunting engine capable of handling the very weighty coal trains along with the mineral and iron and steel traffic of the region. Other work included hump shunting duties. *Trevor B. Owen*

Left: Photographed at Derwenthaugh Coke Works on 23 April 1965 is NCB 0-6-0T No 42. This powerful Kitson 0-6-0 was designed for the steel works at Consett. A Class A loco it was outshopped as No 5 in 1883, further locos being built to the same design by Robert Stephenson & Hawthorn in 1941. This 29ft long loco had a wheelbase of 10ft 9in with the wheels set in front of the firebox and gave a rough ride for the crew when negotiating tight curves. A pioneering design for its day, it had a boiler pressure of 140psi.

Trevor B. Owen

Above: When this view was taken in March 1966 0-4-0ST No 18 *Lewin* was reputedly the oldest standard-gauge locomotive still working in Britain. This outside-cylinder saddle-tank was built in 1863 by Stephen Lewin & Co of Poole in Dorset and was required for shunting and repair work at Seaham Harbour in County Durham. It was acquired from the Londonderry Railway in 1900 and survived dieselisation of the coal staithes in the area because of weight restrictions on the wooden pier and quayside lines over which it worked. The Londonderry family

owned numerous small pits in the Rainton and Pittington areas, coal being carried to the nearby River Wear over early waggonways. Instead of building a line to Sunderland, it was decided to make for the nearest point on the coast which was Seaham, five miles south of Sunderland, the first coal being shipped on 25 July 1831. Seaham also had the last gravity rope worked incline in County Durham and was finally used to send colliery waste to the harbour for disposal.

Alan Jarvis

A fine view of Class Q6 0-8-0 No 63343 as it leaves the shed at West Auckland on 21 August 1962. The northeast had some of the most dilapidated sheds in Britain until the very end of steam despite the redevelopment that took place at Thornaby. Whilst the NER depots were built to fine standards, they were old by 1923. The depot at West Auckland had closed in April 1931 when the Tebay mineral traffic had been handed over to Darlington men. However, on 8 July 1935, Shildon and Wear Valley Junction sheds were closed, the work reverting to West Auckland, which was reopened.

Ken Fairey

Class V3 2-6-2T No 67620 emerges from the tunnel under Mowbray Park at Sunderland with a parcels train for Newcastle on 12 August 1963. When the NER opened a line from Ryhope Grange Junction with a new station on the present site, the first ticket was sold from Sunderland Central station at the north end by William Forster on 4 August 1879. On 31 October 1965, when that office finally closed, his great-grandson, James Forster, sold the last. *G. M. Staddon*

Left: Inside the roundhouse at Sunderland MPD these J27 0-6-0s have been cleaned up for their final duties by members of the MNA enthusiast group on 9 September 1967, this being the last day of BR steam operation in the northeast. Introduced as NER Class P3 in 1906, the design of this class was perpetuated until 1923, the last 10 coming into service as LNER engines.
Paul Riley

Above: A delightful portrait of the now preserved BR Class Q6 0-8-0 No 63395 as it bathes in the late evening sunshine outside Sunderland South Dock MPD during the last week of BR steam in the northeast in September 1967. No 63395 was to become the sole survivor of this class of 120 engines having been turned out of Darlington works on 2 December 1918. The engine never ventured far from its native northeast, being allocated to Blaydon, Newport, Darlington, West

Hartlepool, Selby, Consett and finally Sunderland. Towards the end of steam in 1965, No 63395, together with No 63357, were both out of traffic at Consett with major defects, the former needing a replacement tender and the latter with cracked main frames. It was decided to give No 63395 the tender from No 63357, No 63395 receiving some extra repairs at Gateshead to stay in traffic.
R. Hobbs

52 An everyday scene at Wearmouth Colliery, Sunderland, as NCB No 3 shunts a rake of wagons in 1963. This locomotive, built as Works No 7689 by Robert Stephenson & Hawthorn in 1951 was supplied new to Dorman Long steelworks at Lackenby on Teesside. It was sold to the National Coal Board in December 1962, operating at Wearmouth Colliery until it was scrapped in February 1968.

K. H. Cockerill/J. W. Armstrong Trust Collection

Former WD 2-8-0 No 90348 heads an up freight through the station at Monkwearmouth, Sunderland, on 29 July 1967. A most imposing structure from the outside, the station at Monkwearmouth was opened on 19 June 1848 and over its life has altered little, although until the bridge over the Wear was opened it was a terminus. Today the station survives as a museum and in 1974 was awarded the £1,000 second prize in the National Heritage Museum of the Year. Inside, the central features are the restored booking office and the platform gallery which overlooks the Newcastle to Sunderland railway.   *G. M. Staddon*

Left: The squealing of coal empties fills the air at Ryhope Grange Junction on 25 March 1967 as Class J27 0-6-0 No 65833 skirts the North Sea coast with a Sunderland to Silksworth colliery train. At Ryhope Grange Junction, on the outskirts of Sunderland, goods lines to the docks continue straight ahead while the lines to Sunderland station turn off northwestwards. Originally the two goods lines were to the termini in the South Dock area of Sunderland until the North

Eastern station was closed on the opening of the new station on 4 August 1879. When the line nears Sunderland it threads through a 860yd long tunnel beyond which the line from Durham trails in on the left. The old line which passed over the tunnel was used by locomotives travelling to and from the depot in South Dock. When the curve into the new station was opened the old station at Fawcett Street, east of the junction, was closed.   *Trevor B. Owen*

Above: Tender-first Class J27 0-6-0 No 65882 heads past Ryhope with coal empties for Seaham in July 1967. Sunderland MPD's 'Q6' 0-8-0s, WD 2-8-0s and 'J27' 0-6-0s were primarily used for carrying coal from the mines to power stations and the docks although prior to the introduction of DMUs in about 1960 a number of Class A8 4-6-2Ts and Class G5 0-4-4Ts had handled local passenger work.

Derek Huntriss   55

Left: On the final day of steam operation on the Silksworth branch, 8 September 1967, Class J27 No 65894, suitably adorned for the occasion, heads a rake of empties for Silksworth Colliery. Approximately six miles south of Sunderland, the steeply graded branch to Silksworth Colliery became a popular venue for photographers who visited to record the spectacular efforts of the ageing Class J27 0-6-0s.

The first rail link to reach Silksworth Colliery was opened in 1871 and was maintained by the Londonderry Colliery group which provided the connection to the coastal route. This route was later sold to the NER in 1920 and it was not until that year that a second rail link was provided by the Lambton & Hetton Colliery Co from Silksworth's western end into the 1822 Hetton Railway. From 1900 the line had been worked under contract by the NER and because of the steep grades (mainly 1 in 60) the powerful 'J27' 0-6-0s had been used almost exclusively for the last 30 years of steam operation. *Paul Riley*

Right: Once again No 65894 is seen hard at work on the Silksworth branch, also near the end of steam operations in September 1967. She was the last member of this numerically large class to be constructed and appeared as No 2392 under the LNER in 1923 to become No 65894 at Nationalisation. After spending what might have been its last years working from Sunderland South Dock for service on mineral lines in the area, the locomotive was withdrawn in September 1967 and sent to Tyne Dock with other members of the class for storage.

One year earlier the North Eastern Locomotive Preservation Group had been formed to save a 'J27' and a 'Q6' 0-8-0. No 65894 had been chosen as the 'J27' representative because it had been given a new, 1958, boiler in 1963, on being desuperheated. The locomotive was bought by the group in December 1967 and, with the help of the ARPS, restoration work began at Tyne Dock. *Roy Hobbs*

Class Q6 0-8-0 No 63435 departs from Vane Tempest colliery with coal for Sunderland in March 1966. The first of the NER 0-8-0 designs was conceived at the turn of the century when there was a need for more powerful locomotives than the large boilered Class J26 and J27 0-6-0s. Wilson Worsdell's pioneer Class T emerged in 1901. Bedecked in fully lined out passenger green livery with copper capped chimney, polished brass safety valves and North Eastern Railway coat of arms on the centre sandboxes, it was one of the most ornate mineral locos ever produced. Eventually 90 locos of this type were produced, 50 with slide valves and 40 with piston valves. Upon the retirement of Wilson Worsdell in 1910, his successor Vincent Raven developed the 0-8-0 design even further, introducing in 1913 the first superheated 0-8-0s which were to form the Class T2, later designated by the LNER as Class Q6. *Alan Jarvis*

The now preserved Class Q6 0-8-0 No 63395 tackles the climb up Seaton bank with empties for South Hetton colliery on 31 August 1967. Had a letter from BR to the NELPG dated 5 December 1967 been acted upon the preservation of this engine might not have occurred. It read 'Locomotive No 63395 together with other locomotives has been disposed of by competitive tender and I regret is not available to you'. After No 63395 had been scheduled for towing to the scrapyard of Hughes Bolckow at Blyth the crew rostered to accompany the engine did not report for duty. Whether this had something to do with Newcastle Brown Ale is not known but, with BR's approval, Hughes Bolckow agreed ro resell No 63395 for a price of £2,300.

Peter J. Fitton

Left: In the final week of BR steam operation in the northeast, Class J27 No 65879 climbs Seaton Bank with coal empties for South Hetton colliery. Other duties for members of the class at that time included workings to Tees Yard, Dunston and Silksworth. By the end of November No 65879 had been scrapped by Thomson's of Stockton. *R. Hobbs*

Above: Class Q6 No 63395 is seen in action once again on Seaton Bank. This time, in August 1967, it is about to pass Seaton Crossing with empties for Hetton Colliery. The cars of chasing photographers on the right of the picture include the famous Mark 1 Ford Zephyr, RDU 290, owned by the late Paul Riley. Following preservation, No 63395 was first moved to

West Hartlepool roundhouse, and then in 1969 to Thornaby shed. During the next 15 months the boiler had 30 two-inch tubes, vacuum brakes fitted, and a hydraulic boiler test. Restored initially in BR livery, the 'Q6' was first steamed on 18 October 1969 — a day everyone involved with the restoration will long remember. *Paul Riley*

Class A8 4-6-2T No 69855 is seen at Eaglescliffe with the 'Northern Dales' railtour on 4 September 1955. This tour, run by the Manchester Locomotive Society and the SLS, had started from Manchester (Victoria) behind 'Compound' 4-4-0 No 41102, which ran via Blackburn, Hellifield, Clapham and Low Gill to Tebay. From Tebay to Darlington Class J21 0-6-0 No 65061 piloted Class 2 2-6-0 No 46478. No 69855 was used for the journey along the Fighting Cocks branch to Eaglescliffe and thence to Northallerton. Then

No 69855 piloted Class D20 4-4-0 No 62360 up Wensleydale to Hawes where No 41102 was reattached (with No 62360 as pilot to Garsdale), return to Manchester being via Garsdale to Hellifield and thence via Blackburn as on the outward route. The Class A8 4-6-2Ts were originally constructed as 4-4-4 tanks (NER Class D/LNER Class H1) for short distance passenger work. In 1931 it was decided that it might be advantageous if the class was rebuilt with an extra pair of driving wheels as a 4-6-2T. All 45 were

rebuilt in this manner and proved very successful on the many difficult branches in the north east. No 69855 had been built as a 4-4-4T in 1913, rebuilt as a Pacific tank in 1936, and was withdrawn in 1960.

K. H. Cockerill/J. W. Armstrong Trust Collection

Class A3 No 60081 *Shotover* is seen at Middlesbrough with a special train for Redcar Races on 17 June 1961. Allocated to Leeds Neville Hill (50B) MPD on 6 February 1949, No 60081 remained at that depot until withdrawn on 1 October 1962. Until 170 years ago Middlesbrough was the collective name for a group of cottages on the south bank of the River Tees, its nearest neighbour, Stockton, being a few miles further inland on the opposite side of the river in County Durham. It was over five years after the opening of the Stockton & Darlington Railway on 27 September 1825 that a five-mile branch to Middlesbrough was completed on 27 December 1830. The Middlesbrough extension of the S&D left the main line at what is now Bowesfield Junction and within100yd crossed the River Tees on a suspension bridge. Unfortunately the bridge did not prove successful and was severely restricted in the loads it could withstand. It was replaced in 1841 with masonry piers and cast-iron girders, the original piers and foundations remaining in use until the present day. Today Middlesbrough is a city of great importance in the centre of one of the busiest industrial areas of the British Isles.

K. H. Cockerill/J. W. Armstrong Trust Collection

Above: This scene, rich in railway atmosphere, depicts ex-WD 2-8-0 No 90116 as it heads a loaded coal train past the depot at Newburn, West Hartlepool in June 1967. Behind the train is the alignment of the original West Hartlepool Harbour & Railway Co, which amal-gamated with the North Eastern Railway in 1865. On occasions breakers were known to clear the sea wall at this location, giving an unsuspecting crew a soaking on old open-cab locos. Controlling the layout at Newburn was the box dating from 1912. *Trevor B. Owen*

Right: A view taken at the adjacent depot in March 1966 shows ex-WD 2-8-0 No 90588 moving under the coaling stage. Today the shed and much of the extensive layout have passed into history, only the two main lines and an up loop remain. *Alan Jarvis*

A busy scene at Battersby on 3 May 1958 as crews of Middlesbrough to Whitby and Whitby to Middlesbrough trains go about reversing operations. The loco on the left is Class A8 4-6-2T No 69877. At Battersby there were also extensive exchange sidings, a three-road engine shed, turntable and water tower, of which only the last mentioned remains. Passenger workings west of Battersby to Picton and Stockton ceased on 13 June 1954, the last train being hauled by Class B1 No 61034. The line closed to freight traffic on 1 December 1958 except for the section from Battersby to Stokesley which closed on 2 August 1965. Since that time all trains arriving at Battersby have had to reverse and run into Middlesbrough via Great Ayton and Nunthorpe. After the closure of the coast route north of Whitby in 1958, the Whitby to Scarborough and Whitby to Malton routes in 1965, the Esk Valley became Whitby's only rail link with the main network.

In 1958 there had been as many as 29 trains a day using the Esk Valley route but by the late 1960s this had declined to 12, six in each direction. But for strong local opposition from the Whitby area and from the villagers in Eskdale, for whom there were no practicable alternative bus services, this line would have closed along with the others.

Ian L. Wright

The last day of Middlesbrough to Scarborough services via the coast route through Loftus and Whitby, 3 May 1958, sees BR Standard Class 4 2-6-4T No 80116 with the 4.20pm Middlesbrough to Scarborough service at Brotton, the last through southbound working. Prior to closure, the line after Brotton split to go two ways to Middlesbrough, via Nunthorpe or via Redcar. The latter route was used in summer only and ran round the outskirts of Saltburn but did not enter the station there. Passengers for Saltburn had to change at Marske and catch a Darlington to Saltburn train. The flow of traffic on Saturdays was roughly equal in both directions with holidaymakers, some heading for Scarborough and others returning home.   *Ian L. Wright*

Below: On the final day of Scarborough to Middlesbrough via Loftus workings, 3 May 1958, Class L1 2-6-4T No 67754 is seen at Guisborough. A most unusual feature of this 58-mile route was that for some trains three reversals were necessary, at Guisborough, Whitby and Scarborough. In 1862, when the Middlesbrough and Guisborough line was connected to the Cleveland Railway at Guisborough, the station was left as a terminus at the end of a short spur. All stopping trains ran into the dead-end station, the engine propelling them back to the junction where they set off for Whitby after reversing. When diesel railcars took over between Loftus and Middlesbrough this operation continued until passenger services beyond Guisborough were withdrawn in 1960.

K. H. Cockerill/J. W. Armstrong Trust Collection

Right: Class B1 4-6-0 No 61053 is prepared to depart from Whitby with the 6.10pm to York on 24 July 1958. The working through from Whitby to York only occurred in the summer timetable, Whitby engines normally working only to Scarborough, Middlesbrough and Malton. Except in certain cases their loads never exceeded five coaches, the only exceptions being the workings to York.   *M. Mensing*

Class G5 0-4-4T No 67343 threads the Esk Valley near Sleights with a Whitby to Pickering train in March 1954, a three-coach set sufficing for the winter timetable. George Stephenson was the engineer for this line and his main problems were the climb into the hills and the crossing of the watershed. For the first 6¼ miles out of Whitby the line runs up the Esk Valley as far as Grosmont, crossing and re-crossing the river by bridges which were originally constructed of timber. All the main roads out of Whitby run over high ground and mostly over moorland. There has never been a road up the Esk Valley from the town with a result that in severe weather, when snow and ice block the roads, the railway becomes the only means of communication with the interior. The Whitby & Pickering Railway turned due south at Grosmont and after a short tunnel (the only one on the line) Stephenson's original route surmounted an incline with an average gradient of 1 in 15 to Goathland, the trackbed still being clearly marked today.

J. M. Jarvis

Class B16/1 No 61447 marshals its stock at Scarborough Central on 27 June 1959. Scarborough, the most important holiday resort on the Yorkshire coast between the Humber and the Tees, was served by two stations: Central, of which most was the original structure of 1845, and Londesborough Road, opened in 1908. The former, which had 10 platforms of severely restricted capacity was open all the year round, Londesborough Road was open only on summer Saturdays, Sundays and Bank Holidays. It had one through platform which could hold 14 vehicles and one bay which held 11. Mainly used for excursion traffic, a number of Saturdays Only trains departed from it. During the winter months the large circulating area was used by a local bus bodybuilding company for storing bus chassis and bodies. The main flow of railway traffic to and from Scarborough was via York and Malton, and with only Malton and Seamer open along its route, a continual stream of traffic could be handled without the inconvenience of slow trains stopping at intermediate stations.   *Ken Fairey*

An April 1954 view of Class D49/2 No 62756 *The Brocklesby* at Kirkham Abbey, between York and Scarborough, as it heads an up local. Built at Darlington for the LNER in August 1934 as No 230, the locomotive had seen service at Bridlington, Hull Botanic Gardens and Neville Hill sheds before being allocated to Scarborough on 1 July 1951. No 62756 had received its last General Repair at Darlington in December 1955 and on a visit to works on 30 April 1958 it was withdrawn as being beyond economic repair. Luckily, the last member of the class to be withdrawn, No 62712 *Morayshire,* has been preserved.

J. M. Jarvis

Also seen at Kirkham Abbey in April 1954, Class D49/3 No 62774 *The Staintondale* heads an eastbound passenger service, the abbey being clearly visible in the background. Without doubt the section of line between Kirkham Abbey and Huttons Ambo is the most beautiful between York and Scarborough, following every twist and turn of the River Derwent as it passes through the Howardian Hills. The line was originally planned to go through these hills by means of a 1,430yd long tunnel, but to save expense an additional 1¾-mile was built following the course of the river.

J. M. Jarvis

Left: Having closed to passenger traffic from 6 March 1967 the line north of Harrogate sees an unusual visitor on 30 May 1967 as LMS 'Jubilee' No 45562 *Alberta* heads the Royal Train towards Ripon. The Duke of Edinburgh had travelled in part of the Royal Train overnight from Windsor to Nidd Bridge, the train being diesel-hauled as far as York where No 45562 took over. Unusually, the train included both of the surviving LNWR clerestory brake firsts instead of the more usual power brake van at one end. When the line was closed to passenger traffic as far as Northallerton only the stations at Ripon and Melmerby were still open. Newby Wiske had been closed as a wartime measure in September 1939, never to reopen, Pickhill had been closed in September 1959, Sinderby in January 1962, and Nidd Bridge and Wormald Green in June 1962. *P. J. Fitton*

Right: Fowler 2-6-4T No 42405 is at the head of the RCTS 'North Eastern Railtour' as it leaves Middleton-in-Teesdale on 30 September 1963. The tour had left Newcastle Central behind Class V3 No 67620 which traversed the old main line through Washington and on to Durham for the Waterhouses branch. Continuing via Bishop Auckland and Tow Law, No 67620 hauled the train as far as West Auckland where No 42405 took over for the run to Middleton-in-Teesdale. Ivatt Class 4 2-6-0 No 43129 reappeared at Barnard Castle and worked the train for the remainder of the day. *Roy Hobbs*

Left: Ivatt Class 4 2-6-0 No 43126 pilots BR Standard Class 3 2-6-0 No 77002 across Belah viaduct with a Newcastle to Blackpool train on 12 August 1961. The line over Stainmore, authorised in 1857 as the South Durham & Lancashire Railway, was an extension of the Darlington & Barnard Castle, connecting with the Lancaster & Carlisle at Tebay. Costing over £500,000 and taking some four years to build, it was probably Thomas Bouch's finest work. The viaduct at Belah which had 16 spans and was 196ft high was built using lattice construction, a feature which Bouch favoured on account of its simplicity and its low resistance to wind pressures. However, much of the design was attributed to his able assistant, Robert Bow.

Above: Also on 12 August 1961, Ivatt Class 4 No 43056 stands with BR Standard Class 4 No 76050 at the head of a Blackpool to Newcastle train at Kirkby Stephen East. Closure of the line over Stainmore came on 22 January 1962, low receipts being attributed to the lack of freight traffic generated from the sparsely populated area which it crossed. *Both: Trevor. B. Owen*

77

Above: Nos 43056 and 76050 are seen once again as they head a Blackpool to Newcastle train through the disused station at Ravenstonedale, passenger services between Kirkby Stephen and Tebay having been withdrawn in 1952. Freight over Stainmore had run in four main flows: coke from Co Durham to the iron and steel works in Furness; steel products including pig iron, rail and girders from Workington; limestone from the quarries near Kirkby Stephen and local traffic. Prior to closure, Penrith to Darlington services had been operated by DMUs with through trains in the holiday season between Tyneside and Tees-side towns and Blackpool. A fortnightly train each way between Durham and Ulverston from 1932 to 1962, conveyed miners from the Northumberland and Durham coalfield to a convalescent home near Ulverston in Furness, and occasionally Forces personnel on leave from Broomielaw and Barnard Castle. *Trevor B. Owen*

Right: Former NER Class P3 0-6-0 No 2392 marshals a demonstration freight at Goathland on the North Yorkshire Moors Railway in December 1976. No 2392 had made her preservation debut on 25 October 1972 after five years of effort by members of the North Eastern Locomotive Preservation Group. The inaugural run was preceded by a ceremony marking the co-operation between the NELPG and the North Yorkshire Moors Railway. *Derek Huntriss*

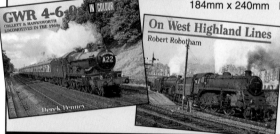